My First Animal Library

Owls

by Martha E. H. Rustad

Ideas for Parents and Teachers

Bullfrog Books let children practice reading informational texts at the earliest reading levels. Repetition, familiar words, and photo labels support early readers.

Before Reading

- Discuss the cover photo. What does it tell them?
- Look at the picture glossary together. Read and discuss the words.

Read the Book

- "Walk" through the book and look at the photos. Let the child ask questions. Point out the photo labels.
- Read the book to the child, or have him or her read independently.

After Reading

- Prompt the child to think more. Ask: Have you ever heard an owl hoot? Where was it? Could you see the owl?

Bullfrog Books are published by Jump!
5357 Penn Avenue South
Minneapolis, MN 55419
www.jumplibrary.com

Library of Congress Cataloging-in-Publication Data
Rustad, Martha E. H. (Martha Elizabeth Hillman), 1975-
   Owls / by Martha E.H. Rustad.
     p. cm.—(Bullfrog books. My first animal library, nocturnal animals)
   Summary: "This easy-to-read nonfiction story tells a "night in the life" of an owl, from waking up, hunting, and feeding babies, to going back to sleep when the sun comes up"—Provided by publisher. Audience: K to grade 3.
   Includes bibliographical references and index.
   ISBN 978-1-62031-071-7 (hardcover)
   ISBN 978-1-62496-071-0 (ebook)
   1. Owls—Juvenile literature. I. Title.
   QL696.S8R87 2014
   598.9'7--dc23
                                         2013004611

Series Editor: Rebecca Glaser
Series Designer: Ellen Huber
Book Designer: Lindaanne Donohoe

Photo Credits: 123rf, 5; Alamy, 6–7, 9, 15, 16, 18, 20; iStockPhoto, 4, 7, 10, 12-13, 23a; Shutterstock, cover, 1, 3t, 8, 11, 14, 19, 22, 23b, 23c, 23d, 24; Superstock, 3b

Printed in the United States of America at Corporate Graphics in North Mankato, Minnesota.
4-2013 / PO 1003
10 9 8 7 6 5 4 3 2 1

Table of Contents

Owls at Night

The sun sets.

Night begins.

Owls wake up.

An owl hunts at night.
It turns its head.
It looks around.

An owl can hear
quiet sounds.

What's that?

A mouse!

The owl follows the mouse.
Its wings are quiet.

The mouse does not hear
the owl.

The owl swoops low. It grabs the mouse with its sharp talons.

talon

The owl flies to its nest.

Its mate is there.

She sits with
the owlets.

owlets

15

Screech! Screech!

The owlets beg for food.

Owls tear up food
for their babies.

The owl roosts
near the nest.

It hoots.

**Hoots tell its mate
it is near.**

The sun rises.

Day begins.

Owls go to sleep.

Parts of an Owl

head
An owl can turn its head almost all the way around.

beak
A hooked beak helps an owl tear up its food.

feathers
Dull feather colors hide owls in trees.

talons
Sharp talons grab prey.

Picture Glossary

mate
One of a pair of male and female owls.

roost
To settle down for sleep.

owlet
A young owl.

talon
A bird's claw.

Index

To Learn More

Learning more is as easy as 1, 2, 3.

1) Go to www.factsurfer.com

2) Enter "owl" into the search box.

3) Click the "Surf" button to see a list of websites.

With factsurfer.com, finding more information is just a click away.